IRIS OF CREATION

BOOKS BY MARVIN BELL

POETRY

Iris of Creation [1990]

New and Selected Poems [1987]

Drawn by Stones, by Earth, by Things that Have
    Been in the Fire [1984]

These Green-Going-to-Yellow [1981]

Stars Which See, Stars Which Do Not See [1977]

Residue of Song [1974]

The Escape into You: A Sequence [1971]

A Probable Volume of Dreams [1969]

LIMITED EDITIONS

Woo Havoc (pamphlet) [1971]

Things We Dreamt We Died For [1966]

Poems for Nathan and Saul (pamphlet) [1966]

POETRY COLLABORATIONS

Annie-Over (pamphlet) (with William Stafford) [1988]

Segues: A Correspondence in Poetry (with William Stafford) [1983]

PROSE

Old Snow Just Melting: Essays and Interviews [1983]

Iris of Creation

 POEMS BY

Marvin Bell

COPPER CANYON PRESS

PUBLICATION OF THIS BOOK WAS MADE POSSIBLE
BY A GRANT FROM THE NATIONAL ENDOWMENT FOR
THE ARTS.

COPPER CANYON PRESS IS IN RESIDENCE WITH CENTRUM
AT FORT WORDEN STATE PARK.

ISBN 1-55659-031-8 (CLOTH)
ISBN 1-55659-032-6 (PAPER)
LIBRARY OF CONGRESS NUMBER 90-81355

COPPER CANYON PRESS
POST OFFICE BOX 271
PORT TOWNSEND, WASHINGTON 98368

Grateful acknowledgment is made to the editors of publications in which the following poems, several in earlier versions, previously appeared:

THE AMERICAN POETRY REVIEW: *Cargo Moving to Gaza (1988)*, *Darts*, *An Elegy for the Past*, *Frankenstein's Monster*, *How He Grew Up*, *I Shed My Blood on Unimportant Battlefields*, *Marco Polo*, *Nature*, *Poem after Carlos Drummond de Andrade*, *Sevens*, *Street Fair: The Quartet*, *3 Horses Facing the Saskatchewan Sun* and *Washing Our Hands of the Rest of America*.

ANTAEUS: *He Had a Good Year.*

THE ATLANTIC: *Comb and Rake* and *Victim of Himself.*

THE BEST AMERICAN POETRY 1990 (SCRIBNERS): *Victim of Himself.*

BOVINE INTERVENTIONS: *The Plague* and *Schools of Little Fish.*

THE GETTYSBURG REVIEW: *The Retaliatarians.*

THE IOWA REVIEW: *After Tu Fu, The Body Breaking* and *Portrait.*

THE KENYON REVIEW: *Initial Conditions.*

THE MASSACHUSETTS REVIEW: *Dark Brow* and *from: The Book of the Dead Man.*

THE NATION: *Not Joining the Wars.*

THE NEW REPUBLIC: *An American Anthem* and *I, or Someone like Me.*

THE NEW YORKER: *An Old Trembling.*

THE NORTH AMERICAN REVIEW: *By the Iowa* and *Tie-down of a Bonsai.*

POETRY MISCELLANY: *The Big Slick* and *A Primer about the Flag.*

POETS RESPOND TO AIDS (CROWN): *The Plague.*

RIVER CITY: *The Bow.*

SEASON OF DEAD WATER (BREITENBUSH): *The Big Slick.*

THE SOUTHERN CALIFORNIA ANTHOLOGY: *Meditation on Dust* and *On Location.*

THE TAOS REVIEW: *Big Day in Santa Fe, If I Had One Thing to Say, Lawn Sprawled Out like a Dog, Ode to a Candle, A Plot, Sweeping Up at Closing Time* and *Tall Ships.*

THE VIRGINIA QUARTERLY REVIEW: *Icarus Thought, I Will Not Be Claimed* and *Language without Miracles.*

WESTERN HUMANITIES REVIEW: *Ice* and *A Man May Change.*

ZYZZYVA: *Spot Six Differences.*

The lines by Pablo Neruda which introduce *Iris of Creation* are from "Sexual Water" as translated by Robert Bly and James Wright. "Ode to a Candle" pays homage to Neruda's *Elemental Odes.*

"By the Iowa" follows the spirit and method of William Stafford's poem, "By the Snake River."

DOROTHY

CONTENTS

I look at secretive dreams,
I let the straggling days come in,
and the beginnings also, and memories also,
like an eyelid held open hideously
I am watching.

PABLO NERUDA

Dark Brow

The dark brow of the creek wrinkles over time
as if something had been born there.
Scavenging all night, the water that runs there
brings things from time past.
Some of these things are the wrappers, the coats,
of what it meant to say, "I tasted"
or "I felt." And this, whatever it is, is not that.

All of us have felt the fatigue of dark water,
the burden massed at yard's edge,
and in the line of the garden
beyond the onions, there are fresh tears.
I do not say we should live forever,
for who could bear it,
only that we should one day enter completely into life.

In the beginning, as at the end, there was nothing,
though "was" is the psychic's verb,
the one that proves the existence of a current
by rising after it has passed
and shaking its head furiously, spraying water.
"I was," we say. "Therefore, I am." We also believe
a piece of us has washed away and may be worth something.

A Man May Change

As simply as a self-effacing bar of soap
escaping by indiscernible degrees in the wash water
is how a man may change
and still hour by hour continue in his job.
There in the mirror he appears to be on fire
but here at the office he is dust.
So long as there remains a little moisture in the stains,
he stands easily on the pavement
and moves fluidly through the corridors. If only one
cloud can be seen, it is enough to know of others,
and life stands on the brink. It rains
or it doesn't rain, or it rains and it rains again.
But let it go on raining for forty days and nights
or let the sun bake the ground for as long,
and it isn't life, just life, anymore, it's living.
In the meantime, in the regular weather of ordinary days,
it sometimes happens that a man has changed
so slowly that he slips away
before anyone notices
and lives and dies before anyone can find out.

An Old Trembling

Often one wonders what the snake does all day in its pit
to so successfully keep away hands
and be left alone like a solitary zipper
encircling some space from which it has squeezed out all
    the light
it would seem,
as if no other creature could so love the dark during the day.
And everyone knows about the kiss of the snake.
And everyone knows about the eyes of the snake.
In its mouth is the blue light of old milk.
On its tongue is a map of red rivers.
It knows your body, your own body, like its own.
It begins with your foot, lurking in a boot,
and ends in the venomous sweat of the heart
if you bother it. But whoever leaves alone
whatever in nature wishes not to be disturbed,
he or she will seem like a god,
so unlike a human being,
even to a snake.

Nature

A hand that tries to shake a hand,
an ear pressed against a silver railroad track,
in a place one goes to be alone
called by various names for parts of the body.
Waiting for this, waiting for that.
Swept by the penetrant odor of choked lilies
and the smoke of dark clouds.
Alone by virtue of a garden. And then
with all five senses about to expire,
suddenly a wedding of male and female
in pools of electro-chemical memory
that existed before dawn,
before thick and thin, before the dead thought.
Earth of dusk. Earth of the belly. Earth of the breast.
And heaven the heaven of a slash
that wakes the sea.
All that is better, all that is worse,
whatever is half-formed,
which is to say everything born one of two parents,
every living thing turned round in the cave,
unable to distinguish the unlit road
from the bright slash in the sky,
shall be set free to roam
to find a husband or a wife
with whom to ruminate
on the messages in the footprints of ants and flies
and on the rights of others, too, who live
a few hours only or part of a day
without once hearing a rooster
scare away an angel.

He Had a Good Year

while he was going blind. Autumnal light
gave to ordinary things the turning
beauty of leaves, rich with their losing.
A shade of yellow, that once stood opaque
in the rainbow of each glitzy morning,
now became translucent, as if the sun
broke against his own window. As for white,
it was now too much of everything,
as the flat deprivations of the color black
moved farther away: echoes of a surface
unseen and misremembered. I must tell you
how he managed as the lights went slowly out
to look inside the top glow of each object
and make in his mind a spectrum of inner
texture, of an essence isolate from the
nervous trembling of things struck by light.
"Ah, if God were only half the man he is,"
he said, "he would see things this way."

Icarus Thought

The nature of a circle prevents it
from ever being a human hand.
And the essence of a rectangle
prevents it from ever being a skull.
Yet important people who can see
for themselves can't get this straight.
So others have to give them a picture
of the moon burning inside a mouth
and worms nesting within a cloud
and an empty sleeve that screams.

One who knows the hollows of a skull
will have felt the remorse of a knife.
And one who truly sees the moon
will know the sadness of the twilight.
But that fool we were in wax,
he will be lifted always by emptiness
and made to embrace the music,
first of the sun and then of the moon,
and learn the ambivalence of doorways
and a dawn that looks like evening.

Victim of Himself

He thought he saw a long way off the ocean
cresting and falling, bridging the continents,
carrying the whole sound of human laughter
and moans—especially moans, in the mud of misery—
but what he saw was already diluted, evaporating,
and what he felt were his teeth grinding
and the bubbles of saliva that broke on his tongue.

He was doomed to be a victim of himself.
He thought he saw, in the future, numberless, cavernous
burials—the outcome of plagues, of wars,
of natural disasters created by human beings—
but what he saw was already faded, disintegrating,
and what he felt was the normal weakness displayed
by droopy eyes and muscles that bleated meekly.

He thought he saw from Earth up to the stars
and from any one moment back to the hour of his birth
when desire produced, in the slush of passionate tides,
a citizen of mud and ash, of lost light and dry beds,
but what he saw was already distorted, moving away,
and what he felt was a sense of loss that so often
he had been at peace in her arms when he did not
        intend to be.

Ice

Strange to see people marooned in parking lots
two feet from their cars, unable to take a step.
The lights go by on the roadway in the overcast.
Another car turns in and slides sideways to a stop.
Each driver is almost killed in slow time,
and the sliding of each car lasts a small eternity.

Then these workers who have much in common –
the end of their lives, for one thing – stand still
as the clock of their days stops and refuses to run.
All over the lot, no one wants to laugh –
it is too cold, too windy – and no one wants to crawl.

Then there is something: a piece of newspaper
to stand on, some rough snow to the side, a hand.
The traffic goes on swishing and gusting. Somewhere
a siren shines on the highway toward a collision,
while here in sight of the door stand the pillars
of this factory community, blue-faced on an ice-bed.

I remember again how long it took to regain a footing
once the car started its slide and a slight lift.
Time took everything back except the milky light
of headlamps unable to let go of their rigorous posture.
Someone would come to find out what had happened.

2

I don't think it, and you don't.
But it's true that the seat belt saves the driver
from the steering column.

And the gasoline that everyone fears will ignite
doesn't go up all that easily.
Helpless, one then has the feeling of living fully.

3

I say that I open my eyes,
but they were never closed, all the while.
The car finds its tires again and stops,
and the other cars swerve past me or stop,
their brake lights flickering as each driver decides
which will be worse. I am alive.
I am alive again and again. The sound of the siren
comes closer, pulsing in the brittle morning air
like the blow of an axe on a frozen river.

Meditation on Dust

If a man's skeleton may burst into flame on the fuel of his human breath, perhaps it is likely that our very Earth may someday grind to a dead halt, unable to nose aside the mounds of dust that have been falling onto its surface ever since...

First the pistons that drive the ball must come to a stop, the oil in the valves crumbled and balled up, so that there can be no movement up or down, nor north nor south, nor away nor toward...

Before Earth is broken, before the pistons slow and drop, there will come that unnoticeable first moment, that minute catch in momentum, that hitch in the continuous releasing of the solar slingshot, when the ballistics of the breath disperse, and the last water in the universe spits against the curves, and the past blows up in a constellation that bears the name of...

Blame the jazz dizziness, the combustible river wind and the halo of dust one gathers when walking through alleys where photographs are still forming out of the long past that...

When a small thing falls, the dust that rises from the instant at the end of its collapse can fill a cavity larger than the thing itself. And when a medium-sized thing plummets, the dust it raises can wrap the Milky Way. But when a truly large thing falls, the dust it displaces flies off beyond our imagining, leaving behind the kind of wax in which everything stops. And this is why some people believe in meteors, and others live by the law that says opposites attract....

Comb and Rake

The comb that we love, of all combs,
is a rake through our private beach,
giving a voice through missing teeth
to all the things one hopes to find in the sand
next to horseshoes, aluminum tabs,
and sand ants thrilled by the sight of a claw.

The rake that we love, of all rakes,
is a comb through our private grove,
singing at perfect intervals
of all the things one hopes to be divine,
here, among human tongues rusting in fire,
bearing the singed hair and beard.

Of all names, the name we most love
mocks an unsaid name we did not love –
in the smallest possible space,
cast upon a screen encircled by a naked moon
at the center of a solar system
where there is only you and me and someone else.

Lawn Sprawled Out like a Dog

When the peacock screams out at night, do you think it knows
its cry makes a man look at himself to see if he is suffering?
Perhaps the peacock and all birds realize
the effect of their voices. They carry a musical score in their
      bones,

which are so thin – toothpicks, really – their only defenses
are the gluttony that puffs them up, the edges of their songs
      and cries,
and the flimsy handkerchiefs on struts
they wave as they fly or run from grass to grass.

Even the tiny mosquito, most blood-thirsty of God's creations,
considering the brevity of its life, must sense the communion
      to come
when, shivering and wild,
with nothing to eat, she sings us to the wood like Circe.

Forgive me, I mixed up the horrible little mosquito, an insect,
with the eagle, the loon and the brave, little sparrow.
Forgive me, I only recently learned
to slap down the gnats that hover near the shores of human
      swans!

Tie-down of a Bonsai

A ladder propped against a rainbow:
We were told that life waited to exist;
death waited to be that which was and isn't.
Language, of and by the living, cannot express
our absence, but readies itself in stitches,
erasures, the dead skin adhering to a bandage,
untellings, retellings, revisions, reversions,
the resonant vacancy of interlude,
the *qua* of music, the held air in the audience
just prior to coughing, the lost vacuum
of a black hole, the nuclei of tears —
it is all a performance, from the tie-down of a bonsai
to the reddening of apples,
from the talk of Absurd Phenomenology
to the passionate kiss,
from angels on the head of a pin to quantum physics,
from the conceptual to the pre-conceptual,
from the environmentalist to the survivalist,
from the garden to the slaughterhouse.
Listen for an introduction to Creation:
a horn sounds in the background,
increases, at first each frequency of the whole
seems like the plucking of a single hair,
but the fog, which does not lift, filters alarm
from the tighter strings, so that we hear a fatherly,
throaty, fibrous drone. And in
the harbors of dust, this trembling of sound waves
begins our story. From the lightest touch,
imprinted in the slightest disturbance,
a history commences that will lead to thunder and roses,
to the beginning of each kiss and to the end of each kiss,
to each particular in a long line of particulars,

every one with its special claim
except when one may stand, as now, for innumerable others,
stranded perhaps past anything we can imagine
unless it be a stone thrown into the dark,
the inside of a sound,
tomorrow a ladder propped against a rainbow.

3 Horses Facing the Saskatchewan Sun

They were yellow, brown, golden, tawny.
They were ropy, sinewy, eels in the hands of the three blind
     men.
They were spirit in the saddle, flesh of belief.
They were posed, they were active, they lived motionless.

Where they stood side by side facing the sun,
where they stood and did not move in the face of the sunshine,
where there they breathed but did not move or twitch,
there they remain in memory and cannot age.

Criminal to tell time to the animals,
brutal to make known one's wish for a change of any kind,
despair to be truthful, cruel to be wishful –
all words to be trampled for the basic right to be.

The Plague

Then all the evidence we have of who is
missing in the general convolution
of what we call our sky, talking prose,
or heaven, hoping now for absolution,

is the white holes in a cloth hung to cover
the corpse of outer space, as dead to us
as the porch light flickering after the foreign movers,
after a labored day, drive off with the bus.

A puppet stage, through whose quivering curtain
we once took note of certain bodily presences,
which metaphor could serve, when life seemed certain,
now falls around the dolls where innocence is.

Many are gone or going. We see the light
that comes from a cold star and know the outcome.
At last report there was more still to night
than stars, or yet to life than heaven and home.

Sevens (Version 3):
In the Closed Iris of Creation

A pair of heavy scissors lay across the sky
waiting for an affirmation,
waiting for the go-ahead of tragic love.
The sky, as always, was full of sobbing clouds
ready to rain down heavily on desire
wherever a hand opens or a leg stretches out
and life waits to begin —
the way everything, even scissors, waits to begin.
We who began in water, in clay,
in the ancient diggings of the word,
whitened by the chalk of dreams,
bloom in colors (everyone has noticed!)
blind toward scissors and clouds.
Within the sight of a pail of water,
our mothers pushed us away
for the good of our souls
into a world where the sun had burned a hole
in the name of love.
Sleep in the sewers
descends, bringing an inner life
utterly at peace behind an in-turning iris —
crawling, pre-cadaverous, fetal.
To choose between knowing the truth
or, on the other hand, orgasm and repose,
always with the patience of a cricket on guard
in case Spring should arrive in disguise,
hiding its muscular body under rags,
its footsteps muffled by the mating of vines —

to choose at all, we have to crawl
on bare knees down alleys of pumice
and plead among the red columns of silos,
in the dust of exploding grains,
with shaking hands and trembling lips
plead for a severing of knives.
If now in the blackest hole we sometimes dance
like an orphan among loaves of black bread,
and lift plain water to our lips to toast
our good luck, and if in a thicket of almonds
with a smell of oil before it turns
to bitter wine,
we laugh so hard we lose our bodies momentarily,
we are also, at the same time, absorbing
the shivering of all cities
born of this baked earth, this chaste diamond
that flowered, reluctantly, absurdly,
into an eternity of ice
and descended through the decorations of the frost
to be shipwrecked in space.
And so each morning I throw a little chalk into my coffee
in memory of the blood and bones of the universe,
and each morning I eat some sacramental bread
as a prayer
not to become one of the thieves
but to save and keep my life for whenever I may need it,
perhaps when things are going better,
when everything is or isn't sevens,
and the planet is in perpetual motion
giving regular birth to the spaces behind her.
I myself swear never to be surprised
when someone elects to stay in the womb.
True silence existed only before there was life
and was eaten in the first rain of the universe,

beaten into piles of grain and no grain
in the first silo, in the first air,
without a place to put a foot down, without an us,
all in a hole
that held (aloft? upside down?) as if in an iris
the thin tracings of the first wax,
and of the first delicate amoebic embracings,
and of the shapes to come when love
began to sever us.

After Tu Fu ("They Say You're Staying in a Mountain Temple")

In the damp evenings of summertime,
I cannot trust my words to reach you.
They drink up every nuance shamelessly.
They are more ravenous than my mouth calling.

In the crusty air of wintertime,
I cannot trust my words to go to you.
They see too well the leafless trees.
They know too well the outcome of love.

In the steady dying of autumn time,
there I know that my words will touch you.
Fall is the shadow season, when we meet
on the other side of the clouds.

I, or Someone like Me

In a wilderness, in some orchestral swing
through trees, with a wind playing all the high notes,
and the prospect of a string bass inside the wood,
I, or someone like me, had a kind of vision.
As the person on the ground moved, bursting halos
topped first one tree, then another and another,
till the work of sight was forced to go lower
into a dark lair of fallen logs and fungi.

His was the wordless death of words, worse
for he remembered exactly where the words were
on his tongue, and before that how they fell
effortlessly from the brainpan behind his eyes.
But the music continued and the valley of forest floor
became itself an interval in a natural melody
attuned to the wind, embedded in the bass of boughs,
the tenor of branches, the percussion of twigs.

He, or someone like him, laughed at first,
dismissing what had happened as the incandescence
of youthful metabolism, as the slight fermentation
of the last of the wine, or as each excuse of love.
Learning then the constancy of music and of mind,
now he takes seriously that visionary wood
where he saw his being and his future underfoot
and someone like me listening for a resolution.

On Location

Blood drips from the eyes of
a woman high in a tree. You can see
this if you get just right on the ground
observing by branch, laddering your look
up the rays of the sun: the crown
she wears who pauses overhead.

Your character wouldn't climb alone
that tree in a movie, the music
telling all who yell to you to hear. But
say you get a chance to be in the film —
a star! — and the Director says "Action!"
looking at you, and everyone motionless.

You might climb, imagining anything.
You could promise yourself big
things, things like being good after
branch three or branch five, where traces
of makeup assert steps to take, and
of course to wash the lipstick off.

Marco Polo

He was heroic, fugitive, in love with the machinery
of the sea, and every song he sang was of the sea.

His smile was golden, and a skeleton's grimace
in the earth, for every smile ends up in a grimace.

In his famous hands, a chisel could whistle,
and in hands such as his, an insect might sing.

He whose chances rode the foaming oceans
toward ivory-hued dresses of a new substance.

Thus, among ashes, a scrawny angel may sing,
from a naked belly, of a delicate emptiness.

2

When Marco Polo set his compass for gold
and ivory, and his dictionary for Chinese,

when Marco Polo set his chisel for a smooth bow
(to stir the waves to foam) and a stern like ice,

when Marco Polo fixed his stare on silky dresses
and the porcelain look of China, and when he had

sailed his scrawny machine to a fugitive corner
of the globe, and the faces of his crew were ashen,

and even the rigging grimaced like a skeleton, why
then Marco Polo landed, and the caged insects sang!

3

With a chisel, he found his gold. And ivory, and ashes.
With a borrowed dictionary, he talked and he sang.

With machinery, foam. With machinery, the fugitive.
With machinery, a grimace. With machinery, insects.

With machinery, a skeleton. With scrawny rigging,
a belly of ashes in a fugitive skeleton. With a chisel,

the gold for machines to carry the burnished dresses
to England, though he himself sang mainly of the gold.

He was the Marco Polo of tea and gunpowder,
devoured by the Oriental machinery of the silkworm.

Tall Ships

The one who reaches the crow's-nest
has to go by way of a boot full of water,
wearing a long rope burn and blue tattoos,
and drinking a bucketful of salt,
and always with an eye big enough to let in a star.

The one who reaches the crow's-nest has to go
by the path of most resistance,
leaving the deck behind with childhood wishes
and climbing from the wide life of floors
to the narrow end of the telescope filled by a moon.

The one who reaches the crow's-nest absolutely
must want to, rehearsing in dreams
the layout of cat's cradles and spider webs,
forgetting all ordinances and averages,
apathetic to the widening embrace of the planets.

The one who reaches the crow's-nest,
the one who tops the mast and the crow's-nest,
has to go up by way of the two hands of a pulley,
by following the fists of the clock to noon,
and by turning his face to the blind dial of the cosmos.

Ode to a Candle

The wax comes
from centuries
of
the residue
of feet
scraping the stone
of pyramids and cathedrals
and bringing
on shoulders
covered with the crusty
discharge
of sunburnt sweat
more stone for the glory
of kings and gods
or whoever
insisted.

The wick comes
from
a vine
underground
tying ancient redwood
trees in the west
with
young willows
in the east
who
have but brief lives to let down
and so weep
and toss their hair on the grass
and sweep away
the curses
of the gardener.

The light
and the flame
come from
the friction between
the edge and the center
of the darkness
but it is only in the dark
that a fantastic
blue vase surrounds
the wick
which stands in oil
like
a tree in water,
a tree struck only a minute before
by lightning.

The beautiful blue vase
containing the wick
of a candle
resembles also
a
teardrop, a shaking
shivering
teardrop hanging
from the eyelid of one of the angels
said to be passing
over us
in the sudden
flickering of a light.

I have seen
the shadow alone
of a burning candle
take the shape of a cat upon a wall,
a cat that
grew and grew
until

it had outgrown the range of the eye,
while
close to the flame
a story for children
spread
over the tabletops
and covered
the windows and the door
and
those who listened
within earshot
could hear
a sudden intake of breath
just as
the candle flared
like a stick
caught suddenly
in a burning platinum forest.

When the light
comes only from a candle,
we are trapped inside its winds, shuddering,
and it comes to be
on some day
our last candle
in
our final room
and, even though many claim
to be making preparations,
rarely
does anyone
offer
any last words.

Thus
among questions of evil, of red,
of sunflowers, of the future,

and all the rest of it,
the candle burns
that was kept in the kitchen drawer
for emergencies
of love or penance,
the two human acts
that absolutely must be undertaken
before the silence
of sleep.

One must also resist the urge
to see the candle
as a symbol, since
it is not directly connected
to the gut of a human being, not spun out
from anything inside us,
although it may be placed by a bed
or glued to a saucer
on a desk
or symbolically stuck in the new snow.

I remember the pitiful solitude
of a single candle
left burning on the widow's nightstand
to light the anniversary
of a death
and I remember the massed grief
of the beds of Catholic candles
and I remember
the happiness of birthdays
and the look of a driveway
in the desert
marked by the glow of paper bags
and the one candle
on the boat
everyone worked to shield

from the wind
and I remember, and I remember,
the faint flickerings of the drowned
tip-end of each wick
as it crumbled slowly downward
like a snake that had tried to stand.

Frankenstein's Monster

—"BIGGER THAN LIFE."

Bigger than the best, but not the best,
who can take history by the throat
and squeeze the steam from the new bread,
turn glass to sand, and grind the gears
of planets to oil and oil to water,
until the earth is rid of that Creator
who dared to make a thing without a soul.

I walked because of Science and a scientist.
I stood because he had it in his thought
that life should come from what is dead,
should turn time back and dry your tears.
I, who was made from brick and mortar,
meant to be inferior, was greater.
Given the parts, I assumed the role.

I am the dark body that cannot rest
free from an hysterical note,
made as I was to symbolize your dread.
Through the magnifying lens of fear
you watch me in your son and by your daughter.
While you disperse in every dark theatre
in streams of light, inside you I am whole.

A Primer about the Flag

Or certain ones. There are Bed & Breakfast flags.
They fly over vacancies, but seldom
above full houses. Shipboard, the bridge can say
an alphabet of flags. There are State flags
and State Fair flags, there are beautiful flags
and enemy flags. Enemy flags are not supposed
to be beautiful, or long-lasting. There are flags
on the moon, flags in cemeteries, costume flags.
There are little flags that come from the barrel
of a gun and say, "Bang." If you want to have
a parade, you usually have to have a flag
for people to line up behind. Few would
line up behind a small tree, for example,
if you carried it at your waist just like a flag
but didn't first tell people what it stood for.

Washing Our Hands of the Rest of America

The water is moving again in the lakes of Central America.
On the surface it is peaceful, but at the bottom
the smallest things move about: sand grains, pebbles,
creatures the bulk of a single human hair
with stomachs the size of follicles.
These are the fingers of the deep effects:
when a body disappears into the water,
shifting ground and brainless flitting things
rub away the guilt and responsibility. Soon enough,
the lake water is fit again for drinking
and the laundry of creatures with the bulk of locomotives
and stomachs the size of bomb craters. Someone writes
to the newspaper to express his anger:
"Nothing is clean. The water here, which was pure,
can no longer be digested. The lake nauseates me.
The doctors say that I am allergic to my own brain.
No, I am allergic to the brains of those who run things.
I am going away now. I will live at home.
You will see me as always, but I will have gone away.
The only thing now is not to disappear."

Spot Six Differences

Hand is moved. Sleeve is longer. Hat is
different. Bone is moved. Gloves are
missing. Dress is longer. Window is
larger. Dog is missing. Nozzle is moved.
Tail is shorter. Country is missing.
Air is darker. Background is closer.
Lines are fuzzy. Shapes are general-
ized. Mouth is open. Dog is hiding.
Air is shorter. Hand is longer. Hat is
missing. Tail is moved. Gloves are
different. Nozzle is open. Window is
brighter. Dress is shorter. Country is moved.
Air is darker. Sleeve also. Bone is missing.
Lines are fuzzy. Background is closer.
Shapes are open. Gloves are general-
ized. Mouth is open. Hand is hiding.

Schools of Little Fish

falling in snow beyond the window,
in bread breaking in cracks cut by steam,
because you can't snap your fingers and hold a pencil
even if today you are the best poet in the house.
No one, no one is around to see you stamp on your brain.
No one can swear that the loaf was whole to begin with
when the invisible knife that remained in the ashes
sliced through the bread no longer in the oven.
How do these things happen? How do fish
enter the flakes of the snow? How do raindrops
house all the components of a man or a woman?
No one knows, no one is small enough to see it.

I live in a nation that can saw into the Yukon,
that owns the art to rescue whales and wolves
but is helpless before the rat that lives in the street
among the homeless, and cannot bring itself
to leave Central America. It has learned the lesson
of the schools of little fish, and its armies travel
in raindrops, in the empty chambers of white bread,
in steam opaquing the pane of a window in winter.
Because no one can hold a pencil and snap his fingers,
there are no records, just misprints in the papers
and smudges in the crowd on photographs where
there was trouble. View the photo the day of repression.
And what will you say of it? Here is the flat photo.
The image lies in a thin layer of emulsion.
If you write on it, the picture rubs off. If you tell,
it is thin words, blood carried by abstract breezes.

You must try to absorb the barbed wire left behind
now used to hang laundry, the tank and propeller

and other trophies of war – extra rice, extra beans.
Even if today you are the best poet around,
you must first invite the barbs to penetrate your skin,
there to wring their wire roses in your blood.
And you must wait until the propeller begins to spin
its way into your skull, clearing the chambers as it turns.
And you must wait for the little tanks to start up
in the ghostly shape of lead gasses rising. Not ready
when needed, now you must not come all the way home
until you can carry your brains in your open hands.

Language without Miracles

I suspect the poet, César Vallejo,
to have been born a corpse in the 21st Century,
and I urge him to seek counsel immediately.
I suspect him of having been a naive interviewer
of the Russian poet, Mayakovsky, in Moscow
in 1928, and a Marxist of the tongue.
I respect him for his large ears and narrow shoulders,
I stand in awe of his dreams.
He preferred that wings arrive in pairs.

Who was the new César Vallejo?
Did he shatter the glass currents of television,
trying to leave his footprints on a documentary?
Or did he pluck the one minor note his whole life
on a single black hair of the beloved?
I believe I know. I believe I can feel
the rough cross-stitching of his peasant blouse
in English, in North America, in 1990.
He believed that God was lonely for a father.

The story goes that God desired a son
and lingered in the future. So difficult was it to know
ahead of time the depth that salt could sink to,
that God made César, and other poets of his Age,
virgin messengers, and gave them a Civil War.
César Vallejo delivered up his innocence
in 1938 to the severed hand of the Spanish Republic.
I record here the elevation of César Vallejo
to the rank of worker. He believed God was sick.

Cargo Moving to Gaza (1988)

A tree donated years back struggles
through incursions of pavement where supplies
are a reason for trucks, and armies
a cause for things. All things have reasons.
Here, they lie at odd angles
to existence. From Space you
might see only rubble in this place, and be
gloomy over peace. On Earth you
might see it the same. Arab and Israeli,
dining on reasons, weighing what life is worth,
deciding at the end of a gunsight, –
what was a vision has become a stare.

Sweeping Up at Closing Time

A broom will flame across a world
of microbes with a hush as wide as
the unknown universe. With a gesture
of arms someone rows back and forth
across a floor, smoothing the waves.

It can be that way for any star hurled
into a larger orbit ruled by some Midas
with plans. Too big to be just Mister,
he can brush us off like God. Listen forth,
maybe this time we'll stay in our caves.

How He Grew Up

He found the corner of town where the last street
bent, and outdoor lights went down a block
or so and no more. In the long list of states
and their products, there was bauxite, rope,
fire engines, shoes, even a prison, but not one
was famous for purposeless streets and late
walks. Often he missed the truth of lists
while gone for a walk, with most lights out
all over town, and no one told him, when he
returned, the ten things it was best to, or
the dozen it was better not to. He knew
the window would be lit most of the night
down at the camera shop, and the gentle
librarian would keep the house of books open
if he stopped by at closing. Up the street he went,
leaving the lamps, each night until he met
the smell of the bay, a fact to be borne home
to sleep, certain of another day. The houses of
friends were dark. He never told, in those days.
Something was missing from the lists of
best and how to and whose town did what.
He figured, when no other was mentioned,
it might be his town at the top of some list:
but it was hard to read things on paper
in the bony moonlight. So he never knew.
People ask him all the time to have been
where what happened happened, that made
the news, but usually the big things happened
while he was out walking: the War, the War, etc.

The Big Slick

No one is empty or innocent.
The black lies on the white lying on the black
lying on the. . . . No one is fit to judge
another's home town, not until
he himself has gone there and confessed.

I did it. You, and you, and you did it.
No one is fit to light the match,
no one may abstain for others.
We don't know how to say what a man needs
until it has been lost. Look:

I bring you the tarry stones, I draw
your hand through the gummy accretions of the sand,
but you don't want that. You want a way
to tell the worm from the fish
whenever you see a picture of the way it was.

Everyone is thirsty.
What have we done to make us so thirsty?
O Captain, my Captain! I see you.
I know the kind of town you come from.
I know the boot in the hull that haunts you.

from: *The Book of the Dead Man*

1. ABOUT THE DEAD MAN:

The dead man thinks he is alive when he sees blood in
     his stool.
Seeing blood in his stool, the dead man thinks he is alive.
He thinks himself alive because he has no future:
Isn't that the way it always was, the way of life?
Now, as in life, he can call to people who will not answer.
Life looks like a white desert, a blaze of today in which
     nothing distinct can be made out, seen.
To the dead man, guilt and fear are indistinguishable.
The dead man cannot make out the spider at the center
     of its web.
He cannot see the eyelets in his shoes and so wears them
     unlaced.
He reads the large type and skips the fine print.
His vision surrounds a single tree, lost as he is in a forest.
From his porcelain living quarters, he looks out at a fiery
     plain.
His face is pressed against a frameless window.
Unable to look inside, unwilling to look outside,
the man who is dead is like a useless gift in its box waiting:
it will have its yearly anniversary, but it would be wrong to
     call it a holiday.

2. MORE ABOUT THE DEAD MAN:

The dead man can balance a glass of water on his head
     without trembling.
He awaits the autopsy on the body discovered on the beach
     beneath the cliff.
Whatever passes through the dead man's mouth is expressed;

everything that enters his mouth comes out of it.
He is willing to be diagnosed, as long as it won't disturb
      his future.
Stretched out, he snaps back like elastic.
Rolled over, he is still right-side-up.
When there is no good or bad, no useful or useless, no up,
      no down, no right way, no perfection, then ok it's not
      necessary that there be direction: up is down.
The dead man has the rest of his life to wait for color.
He finally has a bird's-eye view of the white hot sun.
He finally has a complete sentence, from his head to his feet.
He is, say, America, but he will soon be, say, Europe.
It will be necessary merely to cross the ocean and pop up
in the new land, and the dead man doesn't need to swim.
It's the next best thing to talking to people in person.

The Retaliatarians

The particular had become boring though still
I taught it. Call it electro-chemical fusion,
blame it on Rio or the excellence of a meal,
refer to it in the language of rain or grass,
explain it away in columns on aging, in myth,
use it up in the classroom, deposit it
under the soles of boots as they pass, leave it
under the cedar shingles of the new roof—

The particular had become overwhelming
with its Information Age, with its Time-Shifting,
with its Media Impact and Stress-Management,
with its Retaliatarian jargon. Check back
on a glass of water with its sediment and additives,
dismiss it at the falls flogged by litter,
abandon it by the fallen sparrow, the groundhog,
classify it in the anthologies, remark it—

The particular had become too particular,
too discrete. Twist it in Materialism, distribute it
in Utilitarianism, Network it, Run it, Apportion it.
Push one pixel and watch the whole of it tremble.
Yet live in the overlaps, in the meanings,
and there is time to pass through the eye of a needle,
still time to forget, time to love and disdain.
There is still a child somewhere to be sent from the city.

Big Day in Santa Fe

Little bird comes takes a piece of bread,
all in the sun. Holes unnoticeably bigger
in the rocks in inaccessible cliffs. Big, big
words eaten by events, falling walls.
Sun over eastern Europe, my father
turns in his grave toward the Ukraine.
All in the shadow, necessary to say.
My father in his grave more accessible.
Don't misunderstand: my own effort.
Now we try to understand beyond us
the wall coming down between the Berlins.
And east of both, the torches, the candles,
as the Party dies from simple hunger.
No pride here, but wonder. All in praise.
Tomorrow a big day for the homeless,
with gatherings, experts, with plenty
to go around. Getting up one's strength.

If I Had One Thing to Say

I see words effaced in the footprints of the conquered,
slowly sinking into the earth in a round sort
of way, indirect, like sunlight at night, and I see
the speeches of the conquerors preserved on paper,
hurried to a lead mine in the mountains and buried
deeper than atomic mushrooms, insulated
from firestorm and radiation and residue even if
the world has to wait ten thousand years for Adam.

I see grass growing rapidly in those footprints,
and the earth curving in space, and the lean of all
that holds on, from the laughter of the lone coyote
high up in the night to the wishbone of the kill,
hung head down to drain and every part used
and remembered as long as song, deep as prayer,
with the words handed down through centuries
of naming and telling and there's always another Adam.

I see dust made of the fibers of grass, of paper,
from the rubbings of the dirt, the pumice of dead bone,
from the cells of our skin migrating to the surface,
and I see that the dust will never settle, neither
in time nor space, but in the rain of a thousand centuries
many things clear now to us – impulses at the core –
may come to rest in the form of a thought, and this
may be the way it is already: the way it was for Adam.

An Elegy for the Past

It will be darker soon, colder. You see
the corner where you will turn, and you
turn. The house you think is yours,
the door, wait in shadow to be chosen,
and you choose them, and enter, and slowly
peel the layers off that held close an extra
part of the world: the one you entered when
your planet suddenly expanded. Someone
died, and then the universe seemed larger.
Earth swung a sickle path around the sun.
You saw it all in your mind, apart. You were
quiet, and everything was time. All you had
to do was wait, and everything was time.

I Shed My Blood on Unimportant Battlefields

If I ever wear my red shirt again, and lie down
in one of those pipestone canyons in southern Utah,
I'll be the invisible one. Along a trail
of switchbacks, there will be many chances to see me,
but the only clue will be a little bit of echo
held back when a loose stone hits the canyon floor
from the height of limestone cliffs. It's this
my friend will find: everything as it was. Then,
the red eye of the sun will close
as it passes over my stone red shirt.

I Will Not Be Claimed

When I am happy, nothing can divide me
against myself, and I will not be owned.
The carnation in the buttonhole above my head
passes me and I do not look up to see who.
The armored truck parks by the coffee shop
and I do not notice how many the money bags are.
Even the rapturous smell of a new perfume
reaches me but I do not look up to beauty.

When I am happy, truly happy, nothing
can separate me and I will not be claimed.
I cling to the grass and will not let it go
and the threats of winter do not convince me.
I linger over the last of the bread and coffee
and I do not notice the cook locking his doors.
The bad news and the books about death
are part of what we live for, when I am happy.

But when I am not happy, I am one of those
who is broken down into parts and stopped.
I am the brain of a human being but not a being.
I am the heart of a man but not that man.
I see the cook closing and it feels like the end.
Whether I am to be happy or unhappy, I see
which it will be as of the morning, after waking.
I see the white stuff and the black stuff and decide.

Portrait

1

Without the lightness of the sponge,
without the armor of the clam,
without a look about a ship
at rest on the bottom,
without so much in the sight of eternity,
of which these pictures are but samples.

2

With bare knuckles,
with many trees felled,
with many times in the bottom of the rowboat
pressing my hands equally
toward port and starboard
as the great cruisers swamped us.

3

With the flickering of stars,
with melodies improvised
on a framework of space,
with intervals, with distances to run,
with a God who is the breeze
around my fire.

4

And a bruise in the water,
and swift current,
and half a loaf,
and the zero of the sun,
and a skewed body
and an iron kiss.

5

Among shards of gourds.
In the roar of the pine sap.
With the carcass of a sparrow
and the banner of the dew.
In a smear of history.
In the thrill of a green flash.

By the Iowa

I guessed I lived among the currents of a river
without recognizing the groove it made in sky
because it was the habit of men in a family way
not to follow a tide out or a current away
over to what would surely be an unprotected falls
in the days before all cliffs were flagged upstream.

This river found its length and width in ice
when the famous glacier parked and sank through soil
black for ways of looking that had work to do
and the kinds of rules that draughthorse hooves
impress along the course of what a field can gain
when land becomes home town, the lessons and the days.

Deer turn away from the shallows of this river
that runs out of a wilderness toward a skyline
where even low roofs promise an appetite for rain
awkward for self-sufficient men to wish for helplessly
but muskrat venture with owls and bats
and the catfish come to be by a whisker of evolution.

These banks are what the outside of a curve is
and these bridges are for walking on the water
and these rocks are in the river to originate
new soil somewhere in a well-fed century
this side of glaciers when crops may grow in sand
dry to purpose but patient for success.

That future too records its look on eggshells
ground into the route some new river may run
over these places I peer today to catch my look
in deep surfaces that steadily look back at me
while the river rinses off with upstream water
that began in ice before there was any feeling.

Street Fair: The Quartet

The morning spent itself
into exhaustion moving the clouds,
and the Olympic Mountains labored
to bring forth sunlight, and the sun itself!
Then there was sustained applause
for the big woman who sang the blues,
for the frail, anxious woman
singing jazz that leaped among the furniture,
for the beautiful one,
and for the one with the false hand
planted at the cuff of her blouse
like a cutout of a glove.
And two were white and two were black.

New clouds came,
and some were white and some were black.
The songs of the four women rose into the sky.
And the tune of a speck of sand
was amplified in the center of a seashell
until it was expanded like the bread
inside a slaughtered holiday turkey.
America, a great eagle,
heaped air inside its chest and was proud,
and underneath the concrete on which there stood
the harmonies of four women,
two white and two black,
was the webbing on which the city also stood.

How much was in the great snow-topped mountain
hunkered down below the horizon
behind the singers and their songs
to threaten and survive us! Here, the music

shrouds us with the absolute sincerity of a dream
and the true wordless evidence of touch
that renders the entire body a heart,
a heart bearing the drawn-out pulse of a pearl in an oyster,
so that some dance slowly to the notes and keep low,
and some rise higher like hands unfolding.
It was the best of illusions, worthy of life!
That everyone within the sound of a song
can dance at the same time on the wire of a spider.

The Body Breaking

I have been wiping the clear lens
on the right-hand side
of a cheap pair of reading glasses
and it still has a spot somewhere near the middle
of my right eye.
It is like looking through an opal.
Somewhere there is a world of running rivers
where the light has passed through jewels
onto the rapids of the water
breaking down rock.
I have had a glimpse of it,
an interruption, an optical splinter,
or a bump in the road
unseen except that the wagon shook
and half the world
suddenly opened around a crown of light.
One eye at a time is all of how the bird sees me,
and he can fly!
So what if it's not the glasses,
and maybe it's not an opal.
Still the light has to go through something.
And there's nothing perfect here
that I know of.

Not Joining the Wars

Sometimes there isn't any light when
that flash comes. All day, all night,
you went looking for a spark to
bring daytime to your words, that look
of freshness when things go up fast
and the siren volunteers the town
into the blaze, though nothing can be saved.

Lots of things sound like applause:
the dead hands of leaves in October,
or the slapping of tank treads in parade.
Some people can ripple pages in a book
or pause at length till cheered.
It's hard, waiting it out underneath
others' victories and the crackling leaves.

You are possibly one of the lost ones
by choice. You take no maps, blunder
casually from the path, till deep in woods
(the light is slanted, the footing funereal)
that scent gathers, slowly wrapping each
pore with the smell of scrubbed air, –
and you have gotten clean away.

An American Anthem

Grass, let me sleep, but not on Monday.
Monday is no day for sleeping in the grass.
Rockets returning to work! Baker's bells!
Artificial flowers suddenly extruded from cannon
and all made from scratch over the weekend!
There is the reassuring look from the office window.

Grass, let me sleep, but not on Tuesday.
Already, on Tuesday, there is a hint of the eternal.
My look out the window where I work raises me up
to see beyond the near hieroglyphics of the crowd.
At the dangerous edge of the windowsill, a road
without dimension beckons to a body without knowledge.

Grass, let me sleep, but not on Wednesday,
the pivot of all that is not the Sabbath,
the fulcrum of our economy, the quickness of riches,
a day in between, a day more at hand than any other,
and at its center neither ugly nor beautiful.
With God at one end and love at the other, not on
        Wednesday.

Grass, let me sleep, but not on Thursday.
By Thursday, my cowardice likes meat. I have done
what I have done and know what I am likely to do.
I am by now a secret part of the crowd.
On Thursday, I strike out the words I wrote Monday.
On Thursday, I do the shopping; I take my work home.

Grass, let me sleep, but not on Friday.
By Friday, I have lost the power of death.
Fatigue is gentle. I kick at my glass house:
a gentle lunacy that does the economy no harm.
With one day of rest and one of indolent love,
I may wrap myself again in the bodiless infinite!

The Bow

I felt along the shaft of each arrow
a path toward straw – my only target,
stuffed out of the circle it had come in.
A gift, it had a strange way of saying "Here,"
its only word, sometimes mistaking
grass for the bull's-eye. Even as I drew
back the string, a wound opened ahead.

It was an odd kind of miss, my
inaccuracy, then my steel-tipped wishes
falling in new ways, putting their only word
inside things with quivering and bravado.
On the easel of my target, the colors
sprung leaks, at first just a few. Later,
I learned how to do things.

Now, when I can make a line from any
three things, and see my ignorance
coming before what could have been
hasn't missed its time and not happened yet,
I find an old bow and cheat the string
tight somehow, and let fly. Even without
a target it will find straw, if I let it fly.

Darts

The way the feathers follow the tip of the dart
is the way we can be when the wind's up. To the
docks to tie up the boats, if it's a hurricane,
but once in a while a story begins and a path
changes because a little breeze arrived,
from the howl of a baby, from an open door.

The way of the steel point leading the feathers
is the way we have been in still air. To the
yard to water the lawn, if it's a drought,
but once in a while a lifetime occurs and a door
reopens because a ripping-down wind is born
from the cry of a victim, from a barred window.

The days are not our target, nor the nights.
Wildly and without care, things have no end,
but once in a while when we reach out a hand
something in the air will come take hold of it,
and drag us along, spiraling out of control,
and drop us just as quickly when we let go.

A Plot

I know you wish to be located, before the silence,
you above all. It is a human wish
to be somewhere inside the noise, whatever it is.
It could be the end of the world,
no one cares. Maybe it comes from living
by standing on top of everything – day after day,
hurrying about on the skin of the planet,
knowing that a new mountain is always forming
deep inside a symphony of forces.

You get down inside the wells at construction sites,
trying to hear what's in the channel.
You hover near the pipes of the organ on Sundays,
like a sparrow warming itself in smoke
on the roofs. Maybe it comes from the solitudes,
not the multitudes, of our living.
For once you have been serenaded on all sides
by the rumbling of natural forces,
ideals run a poor second to wanting to feel.

Poem after Carlos Drummond de Andrade

It's life that is hard: waking, sleeping, eating, loving, working and
 dying are easy.
It's life that suddenly fills both ears with the sound of that
 symphony that forces your pulse to race and swells your
 heart near to bursting.
It's life, not listening, that stretches your neck and opens your eyes
 and brings you into the worst weather of the winter to arrive
 once more at the house where love seemed to be in the air.

And it's life, just life, that makes you breathe deeply, in the air that
 is filled with wood smoke and the dust of the factory, because
 you hurried, and now your lungs heave and fall with the
 nervous excitement of a leaf in spring breezes, though it is
 winter and you are swallowing the dirt of the town.
It isn't death when you suffer, it isn't death when you miss each
 other and hurt for it, when you complain that isn't death,
 when you fight with those you love, when you misunder-
 stand, when one line in a letter or one remark in person ties
 one of you in knots, when the end seems near, when you
 think you will die, when you wish you were already
 dead – none of that is death.
It's life, after all, that brings you a pain in the foot and a pain in the
 hand, a sore throat, a broken heart, a cracked back, a torn
 gut, a hole in your abdomen, an irritated stomach, a swollen
 gland, a growth, a fever, a cough, a hiccup, a sneeze, a
 bursting blood vessel in the temple.
It's life, not nerve ends, that puts the heartache on a pedestal and
 worships it.
It's life, and you can't escape it. It's life, and you asked for it. It's
 life, and you won't be consumed by passion, you won't be
 destroyed by self-destruction, you won't avoid it by

abstinence, you won't manage it by moderation, because it's
life — life everywhere, life at all times — and so you won't be
consumed by passion: you will be consumed by life.

It's life that will consume you in the end, but in the meantime . . .
It's life that will eat you alive, but for now . . .
It's life that calls you to the street where the wood smoke hangs,
and the bare hint of a whisper of your name, but before you
go . . .

Too late: Life got its tentacles around you, its hooks into your
heart, and suddenly you come awake as if for the first time,
and you are standing in a part of the town where the air is
sweet — your face flushed, your chest thumping, your
stomach a planet, your heart a planet, your every organ a
separate planet, all of it of a piece though the pieces turn
separately, O silent indications of the inevitable, as among
the natural restraints of winter and good sense, life blows you
apart in her arms.

Initial Conditions

The way the sun will slant,
breaking through the window of the Uptown Café
to light a page from Dickinson or Moore,
may pick up the names of America's heroes
as they appear on street signs –
Lincoln, Lawrence, Franklin, Jefferson, Clay,
Washington and Water Streets –
to imbue history with artistry,
and that, in the spotlight of a metabolic fire
born of solitude in the midst of crowds,
may flatten the raised fibers of ten blank pages.
Black where there was white, and ink
where there was water, is the current on which rides
the deep guttural imagination of an animal,
the ethereal silence of a plant,
the indifferent face of stone and dirt
and the bittersweet knowledge of a man or woman
buried in ecstacy the way light flies from fire.

Have your bacon and eggs, have your toast.
Simmer again the early pinpricks of sensation:
those wordless turns in the amniotic river,
the ballooning, the shaping, the reaching,
and then the glare, the hands,
the separation and all the half-returns and afternoons.
Swell again toward the little world of the child.
Sit on your hands, now,
the adult who can still feel from fingertip inwards.
Mark how it feels on the bench. Note the air
cool in May as it mummifies briefly and moves on.
Live at the end of your nose,
on the outskirts of the balls of your eyes,
at the purge of your mouth. Push out your stomach

as you breathe, let your chest sag to feel bone.
The kneecap that moves like a seashell,
the elastic and the inelastic upper leg—
tuck a leg under your chair.

It is all a spine, from which the leaves of the tree
seem to ask for applause,
and round which the breathing of all life forms
distributes seasons and light. It is ever
a spine distributing the shiver of a ghost
who comes to float from out the fog
these islands, spits, peninsulas and continents.
At the spine-tip end of a leaf
a momentary flame spits from the veins,
the same as the sun sends out a green flash as it dives,
and as the brain may flare
at the end of a spinal message, keeping
in mind every pony stop up the long vertebrae
of calcified civilization,
yet still at the tip end of the earth,
at the farthest reach of a root,
find water in the white dust, and blood in an old stain,
enough to bear the future in the air.

Be your weight. Take your smallest step
from word one, build your home at one o'clock,
when the big hand sweeps it away, build at two, at three
and so on, no more ahead of time than that.
Where grease has touched the corner
of a page, it travels edge to edge, erasing opacity.
Be like oil, sometimes like sand or fire,
blown about but unbroken,
stuff that offers hope to a coughing engine,
to the fouled shore and the frozen.
Watch the honeybee, how little it takes away,
and how often it returns
for the necessity of a queen. You are the bee,

if you are a poet at all, eloping with nectar,
proposing honey, and leaving it stamped into a matrix
of wax, in swarming and smoke to grow old.
I read a page in the café, and read the same again,
and then it begins to grow in size and sweetness.

Now, everyone wants to know about failure.
Mankind likes to come upon the bones of the sparrow
or the flattened hide on the highway,
and return to it as a student of entropy,
noting the white salts that have come to the surface,
the caves eaten by insects, the plucked eyeball.
But I say learn your successes.
Unbend from your studies, let the wind in from the west,
and stay your prayers another hour.
In that hour, that indolence, that dreaming,
an angel may salute you,
the sign of which is a rush of responses
to some small thing on the earth, to which you are noon
on the sundial. In a burst, you must get them out
if there is to be peace, if there is to be
completion, if there is to be the road ahead
which we are all traveling—because love can rub its eyes
and read even the paw marks at road's edge.

I have lingered over a page,
recording in wrongly-shaped letters Americans
going to work on the noisy streets of cars and cranes,
footsoles scraping to hurry, calling out,
electric switches clicking on at the corner
and old neon signs in windows buzzing to expire,
until the last door closed and an arc of silence
hooded the abandoned outdoors.
I appealed to myself not to make food from poison
or blood from water or song from interval,
but to loiter in the vacancy,
waiting for a signal, an inkling, of truth,

and I never had to wait long,
because sooner or later the most horrible things happened
somewhere that brought an ambulance
and a man running down the street carrying flowers
which only a moment's thought could tell me
were too early for a death and must be something else.

And after the refueling, what then?
After the regeneration, with the fog easing upwards
from the prone earth into a dissolving embrace,
and the tide turning tail, its last
washing down the mudflats where penlights of air
sent to the surface by living remains
flicker in a constellation too hurried for pictures.
What of the shark's teeth underfoot?
How goes the tide line of beached seaweed
back to the water? Sit still and see.
Stay at your post, your bridal window into the new day,
resist the urge to begin again, to alter even your shadow,
and so to witness a world unaffected by self.
Steel yourself against the delusion at the bottom
of the cup, where the grounds of coffee
may speak in the shape of a dial. It is not a direction
to be at the center of the compass, nor will you be
revealed by wrapping yourself in glass.

If it were not for words, poor words,
I would never have known the wish that things continue.
Let pleasure continue and pain, and bread
and milk continue to spoil, and erosion
go on as before at the joining of wind and rock
and even where a blade of grass shoulders the road.
Let the apple lose its grip in oversweetness
and the honey settle into layers.
All that falls to the ground to be absorbed
may be confused with death, painted with sad tones,
without a thought for the joy of pure pity

or the painter swept by a ghostly excitement.
Each one of us believes he or she keeps watch,
while in reality we are watched. Each of us
believes we are dying, while in reality we live.
Each of us falls into the trap, tearing away
at the sphere which protects and regenerates us,
the one best described by a pirouette or a cartwheel.

And so the wandering canine knows, the mutt,
knows how a hand may curl into a fist,
or the fist unfold, intuits when the meal ends
and leftovers begin, and remembers the doors of largesse
up lanky alleys to the chimney walls of kitchens.
Walk then with such a dog in town, and with the cat,
the one who parallels your nightly reconnoitering
until you stop and squat, surrendering
to its benign approach. How the independent world
loves that which breathes and yet is still,
like the cat, and will rub at the chance of quick love,
cajoling your shoe and trouser cuff,
arching with half a question, perhaps this one:
"Would you, if I...?" and purring like the underside
of a wave that might have slid inexorably through a dream.
It is a dream to be a human being, cast here among
the dreamless days of cats and dogs,
carrying the burden of their mute imagination.

By animal methods, no need to deny,
and only by animal methods, we have understood
the timelessness of our lives. By sexuality,
we have unlaced the proper shoetops, the stitched waters
of history, and then the lines of entanglement,
the cuneiforms of emotions, the ciphers of agreements,
and found there is a flavor, an odor,
a hope on the edge of uncontainable sensation,
a taste of blissful agony, poised on the head of a pin,
emanating from our bones, a singing wire—

that tight, that tense, that stretched to its limit
and then shattered – the ends pulled apart
now limitless in the distance spreading between them,
the torn tips of the last exposed fibers
splayed, letting go, catching each other as they fall,
creating random sparks that fall to the ground
like bits and pieces of some lost moronic code
staggering, exhausted, into the future.

The report we await goes well beyond the outer rim,
leaping like the vague shape of climax
past the short grasses at the edge of the bluff
that appears after heavy exertion
as an unseen clarity, the sure feeling that if one opened
one's eyes, and screamed, there would be a limit,
a panel, a backdrop to mark the event. So much have we
been certain, that much have we been pulled
by the next horizon, and the next,
leaving echo after echo. The report we await
is yours to make from the bottom of time,
from the place behind the last, narrowed bits of light,
where sound sucks up sound, the corporeal
equivalent, the adult version of what the child knew
who tumbled into the well, and lay for days
underneath the big story, being of households and news
but to itself the absence of the world
into which it would again be born someday, unabandoned.

If it were not so, memory would serve.
But we have found nothing, and science likewise,
to locate presences of life in long fibers of ink
carried by a heart, nor in the lengthy recitation
of presidents engraved within a street plan, nor in a flair
for the names of battles or the dates of books or yet
in a penchant for destinations and right answers.
Deaf Beethoven in his last quartet better serves.
Where is it, that such sound ends in clarity and calm?

Is it in the mind, in the heart, in the stomach,
in the liver, the reproductive organs, the limbs?
Is it in the pulse and travels through us? Is it on the skin,
absorbing and radiating, warming and chilling? And, too,
how have we known the feeling—sitting, listening?
Such questions are like a harbor of twilights.
They lead us into the valley of unanswerable nights.
They decline, they evade, they ride at anchor
beyond the reach of the pier, a harp to the wind.

Memory is pre-history. Remember, if you can,
the net into which you fell in the pre-conscious dawn,
its gridwork, arrayed along a horizontal figure 8.
The whole of it is here today, in this historical town.
Condense your past, squeeze recurrent dreams,
and look also among the residues of dirt and water,
in the lingering odor of fresh bread, in mold,
and in that which drifts your way from rumor
and idea, from under the forehead of abstractions,
those thunderous proclamations of the mind's eye.
In little words is sewn an elemental red thread
that holds together old shoes and new philosophies,
cats and dogs, the first and last steps of a stairway,
the careful fugitive and the accidental isolate.
All that was is here, pouring into this moment,
which offers you every chance for tears. But forget,
if you can, all that has gone through the mystic's cloth,
and spot what disturbs the air with heavy laughter.

Hear it in the cathedral burned into a redwood,
in the fluid gear turning the beacon
at the top of the lighthouse, its light bobbing above
thirteen miles of fog and tidal signatures. See it,
when you can, in the filmy stem of Indian pipe,
devout to fungus but deathly when plucked,
though it takes a day or more to gain that burnt look.
After the blaze that rode the trees and seemed

to keep the sky at bay, in the fresh death of the muck,
legions of fireweed strode the blackened soil,
throwing their youth out while the old ones slept.
You live because a glacier melts, a forest dies,
an animal somewhere falls to its knees,
and you would see in the night face of the owl
a feline curiosity, independent in judgment,
quietly paying out the night to survive. Once again
night's force has unraveled, its harpoon
lying in a vague acreage of water after feeding.

So many follow the weather, and rehearse it,
riding an impending high like vacationers
and wallowing in crusty lows like bean farmers.
Standing out at dusk, sweeping the last solar wink
over the horizon, throwing back our heads
to fit—lens and shutter—up against the concave
camera obscura overhead, we let go, finally, if only
we stay to look up, the false evidence of edges
and distances where once the commonest objects fit.
Where now does an umbrella belong, or a coat?
The weight of a machine tilts it absurdly
underneath the violent ramshackle orders of a galaxy.
Now the explosion at the heart of a star
walks the beams of the past, now a fiery arrow
rounds the curve, braiding itself in flame. But a rose
might be pictured where a single thread expires,
and the whole head of a flowering mountain ash
turns out to be a nest of stars at a low level of heat.

Miraculous to be alive in a tungsten universe,
to count the windows and change our point of view
according to their shape and location, and ourselves
as well, marked in secret by the birth of each idea,
welcome to men and women but not all,
revising and refuting our gods, burning in the fall,
but first gathering the leaves, and then irresistibly

flinging ourselves into the piles,
sometimes having to do it at the length of the rake
because men and women must fast more than children
to reach the next meal, and because of such things
as give each person a feeling
for the souls of those who knew kisses but few words,
and those who said little but laughed easily,
and some who trembled from the beginning to the end
as if they were connected at both ends
to opposing charges and were fated to be incinerated
where others carried torches with impunity.

When the time comes that you walk inside a cloud,
where others may sense, but not see you,
and you as clear to yourself as ever, charitable
to the lack of visibility, adoring the fog, silencing
desire, flinging your sense of yourself from guidance,
lingering in the great freedom of invisibility,
then inevitably the cloak burns,
and you may be told not to walk on the grass.
The wilderness of the mind comes down to a ranger,
a file of pressed flowers arranged by color,
and the deer who crowd from the trees to lick
the antifreeze of automobiles. When you were inside
the cloud, and your feet rocked slightly with each step
on the watery land, were you (tell us) as alone
with your eyes open as ever you had been asleep?
Here then is a use for the blows of a pencil-point
against the grain of a page. At impact, a purity
is born from the attraction and repulsion of an instant.

One must be fond of the mud road, of boats
with names that itch to flaunt the pulse that wrote them,
of beachcombers, of detectives gone to birding,
of the beautiful handles of hand tools, of dropped coins,
of propellers and sudden rainbows, of distant ice fields
and glacial streams, of tide pools, of house pets,

of gardens and clotheslines and mintweed by doorsteps.
One must be fond of these things,
as of empty churches and old schoolyards in long grass,
because love, even light love, reaches back
and picks up what others held, one way or another,
long after a dig is emptied of pots and bones and teeth.
Out of such fondness, the telling. The blaze
of a face that would tell us washes the yellow light
of after-midnight, the conversation continues,
and the table spreads to include long-missing friends,
presidents, explorers, those who left or returned
and have not been deserted, whether or not they know.

To be located, as here, at the table of one's examples,
to have for the moment the unmasked,
the everyday, and all of it having slept in the dark,
diving near a dream reef with as many hand holds
as a sponge has openings, where easily
one might have stood fatally upon the dreaded stone fish
or been poisoned from being hauled up too quickly—
these then are one's "particulars." I know,
time has overtaken the deciduous, as night again
will paralyze the open eye, and our sodium street lights
will rub and rub the open wounds, the doomsdays,
the little edge that pebbles give to the sound of steps
and spittle gives to song. I know,
all this too will pass, and may have passed already,
but still I address you where last you were seen
and, whether or not you understood chaos
or sensitive dependence, whether or not you felt
the synchronicity of our lives, there is no one else to.

Drink what remains of your coffee, close your book.
Is it possible that we no longer see ourselves
reflected in open theatres,
no longer exist by the grace of lowered cannon
or can be said to have vanished

because a cloud came, or a fog, or death? Let it
now be decided if the rain must be too heavy
for the certainty of charity. Or if we are made of ash.
Or if sufferance has blistered its skin of paint
on the sides of unconquerable mountains. The moon
that drew us to its scent, only to be faceless,
is the cache of our romance, but also a truth that spills
into the faults of the mind, depositing a dewy light
where the shapes of animals, living and extinct,
hover in some wounded swamp from which,
when we fully awake, we see the imagination rising,
cloud-like, slowly lifting and thinning out,
resembling a gifted child's version of a ghost.

Spring–Summer, 1989
Port Townsend, Washington

MARVIN BELL was born August 3, 1937, in New York City and grew up in Center Moriches, on the south shore of eastern Long Island. At 22, he left the east coast for Chicago. In 1965 he moved further west to Iowa City, Iowa, and since 1985 he has divided his time between Iowa City and Port Townsend, Washington. His literary honors include the Lamont Award of the Academy of American Poets for his first book, Guggenheim and National Endowment for the Arts Fellowships, prizes from *The American Poetry Review, Poetry* and *The Virginia Quarterly Review,* and Senior Fulbright Appointments to Yugoslavia and Australia. Mr. Bell has taught at Goddard College, the University of Hawaii and the University of Washington, and is currently Flannery O'Connor Professor of Letters at the University of Iowa. His seventh book of poetry, *New and Selected Poems,* appeared from Atheneum in 1987.

The type in this book is Sabon,
which was designed by Jan Tschichold.
Composition is by The Typeworks,
Vancouver, British Columbia.
Tree Swenson designed the book,
which was printed and bound by
McNaughton & Gunn, Lithographers.